Scavengers and Junk Eaters

Contents

Written by Paul Reeder

What Are Scavengers and Junk Eaters?

Scavengers are animals that eat the dead and rotting bodies of other animals. These rotting bodies are called carrion. Scavengers can also be junk eaters. Junk eaters eat garbage left by humans.

From time to time, even animals such as lions and eagles are scavengers. If they cannot catch their own food, they search for food that is already dead.

Some people think that because scavengers eat dead animals and garbage they must be dirty and spread diseases.

Unlike these people, scientists think that scavengers are useful. Rotting meat contains germs that could cause sickness. By eating the meat of dead animals, scavengers help stop diseases from spreading.

Vultures

Vultures are scavengers – they eat dead animals. But vultures can also be junk eaters – groups of vultures will search for food on human garbage dumps.

Description

Vultures live on every continent, except Australia and Antarctica. Most vultures are brown, black, or white, but some also have a mixture of red, yellow, and orange feathers.

Vultures have long, wide, strong wings for flying and gliding. They fly very high in the sky and use their large wings to glide and soar on air currents. All vultures have very good eyesight, and they can spot carrion from high in the air.

Vulture gliding

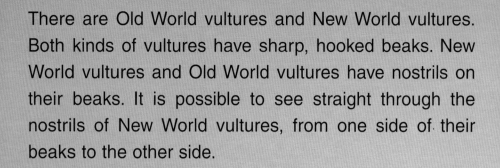

There are Old World vultures and New World vultures. Both kinds of vultures have sharp, hooked beaks. New World vultures and Old World vultures have nostrils on their beaks. It is possible to see straight through the nostrils of New World vultures, from one side of their beaks to the other side.

All vultures have sharp claws called talons. They have four talons on each of their feet.

nostril opening

sharp hooked beak

talons

New World vulture

Old World vulture

Most vultures have bald heads. Some vultures have bald necks as well. Vultures' necks are long and thin, and they use them to get into the bodies of dead animals. Neck feathers would be hard to keep clean, and germs from the dead bodies could live in the feathers.

Vultures feeding on carrion

Location

Old World vultures live in Europe, Africa, and Asia. New World vultures are found in North and South America.

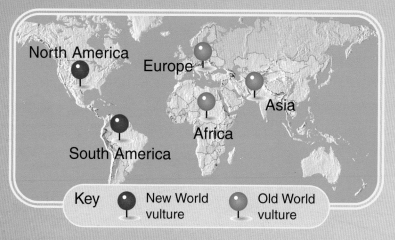

Location of Old and New World Vultures

North America

Europe

Asia

Africa

South America

Key — New World vulture — Old World vulture

Food

Vultures eat carrion. They often can be seen near roads eating animals that have been hit by cars. They sometimes kill animals that are sick or weak, such as newborn lambs.

Vultures also eat junk and garbage, especially if they live near humans.

Friends and Enemies

People have often been the enemies of vultures. The biggest danger that vultures face is the spread of towns and cities. Many vultures are killed when they fly into power lines. Others are shot or poisoned.

Some types of vulture, like the Californian and Andean condor, are endangered. There are not many of these vultures left in the wild.

People have also been friends to vultures. Californian condors were almost extinct a few years ago. To save the species, scientists caught all the wild Californian condors and began raising them in captivity. The condors that were raised in captivity are now being released back into the wild.

Vultures nesting

Striped Hyenas

Like vultures, striped hyenas are scavengers and junk eaters. They like to eat carrion, but they will eat anything they can find.

Description

Striped hyenas have yellow and brown coats, with black stripes. These coats help them blend in with their surroundings. They blend in with the brush where they live. This makes it hard for other animals to see them.

Most striped hyenas are about 3 feet (91 cm) long. They can be up to 2 feet 6 inches (76 cm) tall, and weigh up to 88 pounds (40 kg). The front legs of striped hyenas are longer than the back legs.

Striped hyenas have a lot of hair on their necks, backs, and tails. They have large, pointed ears and thick, strong necks. They need strong necks so that they can carry dead animals to their dens. Their teeth are very big, and their powerful jaws can crush bone.

Location

Striped hyenas live in Africa, and in Asia from Turkey to India. Many are also kept in zoos. People have learned a great deal about striped hyenas by studying the ones that live in captivity.

Food

Striped hyenas eat carrion such as dead zebras, wildebeest, deer, and many other types of animals. People who live near striped hyenas say that they also eat garbage. Sometimes they will hunt live birds, insects, reptiles, goats, or sheep. They will even eat fruit.

Striped hyenas sleep in the daytime and look for food at night. Their good sense of smell helps them to find dead animals in the dark.

Some of the Foods Striped Hyenas Eat					
Hunted	birds	insects	reptiles	goats	sheep
Scavenged	dead animals		garbage from humans		
Other	fruit				

Friends and Enemies

Striped hyenas are the rarest kind of hyena. The most common is the spotted, or laughing, hyena. People are the main enemies of striped hyenas. Like vultures, they are killed by farmers who think that the hyenas prey on their animals. People have killed so many striped hyenas that there are not many left in the wild.

Striped hyena

Tasmanian Devils

Like vultures and striped hyenas, Tasmanian devils are scavengers and junk eaters. Like striped hyenas, but unlike vultures, Tasmanian devils are nocturnal – they sleep during the day and look for food at night.

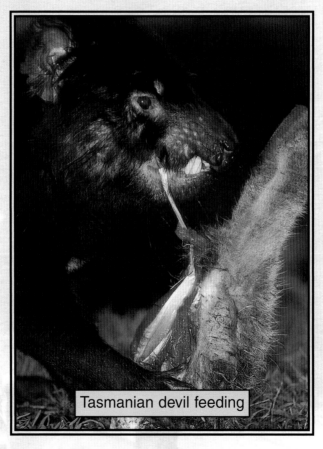

Tasmanian devil feeding

Description

Tasmanian devils are about the size of small dogs. They have large, flat heads and short, bushy tails. They are black, with some white on their backs and chests.

The male Tasmanian devils are bigger than the females, and can weigh up to 26 pounds (12 kg).

Tasmanian devils have very sharp teeth. They also have pink ears, which turn purple when they are angry.

Angry Tasmanian devil

Location

Tasmanian devils are found only in Tasmania, an island off the coast of Australia. Hundreds of years ago, Tasmanian devils also lived on the Australian mainland.

Location of Tasmania

Australia

Tasmania

Food

Tasmanian devils eat insects, fish washed up on beaches, birds, and small mammals, such as wallabies, possums, gliders, and wombats. Sometimes they eat sheep, chickens, and cattle. Tasmanian devils sometimes kill small animals, but usually eat animals that are already dead. They also eat garbage left by humans.

Friends and Enemies

People were once the main enemies of Tasmanian devils. Farmers hunted them because they sometimes preyed on small farm animals. The farmers were paid money for each Tasmanian devil that they killed.

People are now friends of Tasmanian devils. Because Tasmanian devils are a protected species and it is against the law to kill them, they are now very common.

Group of Tasmanian devils

Common Ravens

Like vultures, hyenas, and Tasmanian devils, common ravens are scavengers and junk eaters. Like vultures, they are birds that feed during the day. Common ravens are also like vultures and hyenas in that they feed on the garbage left by humans.

Description

Common ravens are large, black birds. They belong to the same family as crows, magpies, and jays.

Ravens have wedge-shaped tails, shaggy feathers on their necks, and a wingspan of 4 feet (1.2 m). Their 3 inch (7.6 cm) beaks are very strong. The male birds are bigger than the females.

Common ravens are very intelligent. They talk to each other using a lot of different sounds, and they can copy sounds that they hear. Ravens also like to play games, and pairs of ravens will soar and dive high in the air together. Male and female birds stay together for life.

Common raven feeding

Location

Common ravens are found in Europe, Asia, Africa, North America, and some parts of South America. They can live as far north as the Arctic.

Food

Common ravens eat almost anything. They are mainly scavengers, feeding on carrion. They also like maggots and beetles, reptiles, frogs, and shellfish. Like vultures, they prey on sick, weak, or newborn animals. Sometimes they steal food from wolves or birds of prey.

Common ravens are also junk eaters, and like other junk eaters, they can be found near garbage dumps. They also fly over roads looking for animals that have been hit by cars.

Friends and Enemies

Common ravens' main enemies are people, but people are also their friends. Through history, many people were afraid of ravens, and thought that they spread germs and brought bad luck. Like other scavengers, common ravens have been killed by farmers because they prey on weak or newborn animals.

Now common ravens survive in many places because they get so much of their food from people. In some places, like the Mojave Desert, there are so many ravens that they are a danger to other animals that live there.

Common raven with carrion

African Clawed Frogs

African clawed frogs are scavengers and junk eaters. Like common ravens, they will eat just about anything.

Description

The heads of African clawed frogs are wedge-shaped, and very small. Their eyes are on top of their heads. These frogs have four legs, and the back legs are bigger than the front legs. The back feet have five toes, and they are webbed, which means that they have skin between the toes. The first three toes have claws. The front feet are not webbed.

African clawed frogs are green and brown, and they have patterns on their skin. Their bellies and legs are white, with some yellow. These frogs can be fat, and their skin is very slippery.

African clawed frogs have a very good sense of smell. They can also feel anything moving close by them, and because of this, they like to live in ponds of still water. If they are in moving water, they cannot tell the difference between the movements of fish or insects and the movement of the water.

Location

At first, African clawed frogs lived only in the African Rift Valley, south of the Sahara desert. They can now be found all over the world. Scientists think that this species of frog was alive at the time of the dinosaurs. These frogs need to live in water. If the pond where they live dries up, they dig down into the mud. They can stay in the mud for a year.

Food

African clawed frogs are scavengers. They eat anything that comes near them as long as it is not too big. Because these frogs have no tongues or teeth, they rip up food with the claws on their back feet. Then they suck the food into their mouths. They like to eat small fish if they can catch them.

African clawed frogs are also junk eaters. They will eat any kind of garbage that they find in their ponds.

Friends and Enemies

African clawed frogs have many enemies. Reptiles and other animals eat them.

People can also be friends and enemies of these frogs. Scientists use them in experiments. They have found that they have an antibiotic in their skin. This antibiotic can be used as a medicine to help cuts heal quickly. Scientists have even taken these frogs into space.

eyes on top of head

front feet not webbed

claws

African clawed frog

Tiger Sharks

Tiger sharks are scavengers and junk eaters. Like common ravens and African clawed frogs, they will eat anything they find. Like great white sharks, tiger sharks are known to attack humans.

Description

Tiger sharks get their name from the black stripes on their backs. These stripes fade as the sharks get older.

large upper tail lobe

black stripes like a tiger

Tiger sharks can grow up to 18 feet (5.5 m) long. They can be blue, green, black, white, or yellow. Their bellies are white. These sharks have short, rounded noses, and their teeth are sharp and serrated like a saw. They use these teeth to help tear food apart. If a tooth falls out, another one grows in its place. Tiger sharks have a long upper tail which helps them to swim very fast.

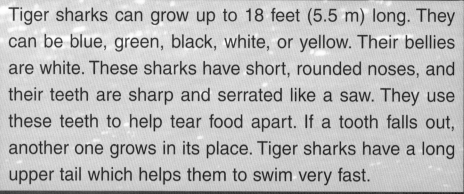

dorsal fin

white belly

sharp serrated teeth

Location

Tiger sharks are found in most oceans of the world.

Food

Like most scavengers and junk eaters, tiger sharks also hunt for their food. They eat fish, shellfish, birds, mammals, reptiles, and even people.

Tiger sharks are such good junk eaters that they have been called the *trash cans of the sea*. Glass bottles, coal, clothes, a drum, and even a chicken coop, have been found inside tiger sharks' stomachs.

Friends and Enemies

People and tiger sharks can be enemies. People catch tiger sharks in nets and on fishing lines, and tiger sharks have attacked people. Swimmers, divers, and water skiers who invade their habitat can be attacked. But many people are also friends to sharks. They are interested in them and work to protect them.

What a Tiger Shark May Eat

bottle

diver

turtle

Scavengers and Junk Eaters Comparison Chart

Name	Kind of Animal	Scavenger
African clawed frog	amphibian	yes
Common raven	bird	yes
Striped hyena	mammal	yes
Tasmanian devil	marsupial	yes
Tiger shark	fish	yes
Vulture	bird	yes

Junk Eater	Nocturnal	Endangered
yes	no	no
yes	no	no
yes	yes	yes
yes	yes	no
yes	no	no
yes	no	some

Index